BERKSHIRE HATHAWAY: AN OPINIONATED ANALYSIS

By

Bala Thiruppanambakkam

Introduction
Berkshire Hathaway : Framework to consider
Considerations for investing in Berkshire Hathaway
Verticals Analysis
    Insurance
        Overview
        Bedrock principle across insurance portfolio
        Analysis of one company in insurance vertical, Geico
        Potential risks for this vertical over time
    Energy
        Overview
        Analysis of one company in energy vertical, MidAmerican Energy
    Manufacturing & Retail
        Overview
        Potential risks for this vertical over time
    Transportation
        Overview
        Potential risks for this vertical over time
    Aerospace & Chemicals
        Overview
    Housing
        Overview
        Potential risks for this vertical over time
    Marketable Securities Permanent Holdings
    Investment portfolio
Investment considerations: Evaluation for investment undertaking
      Generating excess cash
      Opportunity cost
      Capital
      Negative Cost of Capital companies:

These are companies that get money lent/forwarded to them in advantageous terms, provided they are prudent custodians of it, deployment of which further generates additional capital, that can be used for the company's benefit.

Normal cost of capital companies:

Return on capital employed

Business model disruptions in industry

Berkshire: Investment considerations analysis

Berkshire principles and model: A discussion

Sources of Capital: Analysis

    Float

    Cash returned

    Debt borrowing

Return on capital employed

Business model disruptions in industry

Managerial Tenure Continuity

Berkshire Hathaway: How will it evolve over decades from here

INTRODUCTION

Berkshire Hathaway is a remarkable business canvas(unfinished) put together by two extraordinarily able and rational minds over decades.

Intent of this book is to provide a framework for thoughtfully analysing Berkshire Hathaway and then present the company in terms of that. This is a framework that I arrived at after studying Berkshire and refining it over multiple iterations over the last decade.

My primary aim in writing this down was to pass this along to my children, who I hope one day, when they are grown up, will find this to be a useful tool for deeper understanding of Berkshire Hathaway and to analyse it as a continuing concern.

I have put in a considerable portion of my worth into Berkshire and I am hoping my spouse and our children will have the benefit of this investment. I have tried to keep this framework to be useful across time to analyse Berkshire, as I know it will expand into areas presently we cannot even fathom.

Helping me in this process is the fact that there lies an underlying stream of consistent principles acting as a bedrock, in the way Berkshire was put together and a coherence of sorts, which unifies the whole.

I aim to distill and provide a useful tool for those willing to spend thoughtful and intense time analysing and studying Berkshire. I hope other shareholders will find it useful enough to serve as an introduction to Berkshire Hathaway for their spouses, children or extended family members whom they will one day bequeath some berkshire shares.

I do not claim any particular advantages nor any breakthroughs in this treatment. There are a couple of good books if one wants to understand some of the principles and processes of this conglomerate. But the best way to truly understand Berkshire Hathaway, in my opinion, is to read all the annual reports written by Mr. Buffett, in time sequence it was written in. I would recommend serious investors also read Wesco's reports by Mr.Munger in the same way. These two readings supplemented by public writing of Mr.Buffett in various newspapers and magazines(Fortune, WSJ and Washington Post) along with Mr.Mungers speeches, should be enough material for any one seriously considering to understand and/or invest in Berkshire Hathaway.

Hoping that this book would supplement those reading with a view towards evaluating Berkshire. It is intended for people with curiosity for additional understanding of Berkshire, by providing an additional tool in their arsenal. Even if this book provokes a few insights or thoughts I would consider my purpose as served.

I have structured this book like this
- First a framework or theme to think about a company.
- Next I discuss how Berkshire fits in this framework/theme.
- I conclude by adding my thoughts on how Berkshire Hathaway could evolve.

A note on my framework for thinking about a company. As with probably every other shareholder of Berkshire Hathaway, I have read and benefitted by the thoughts shared by Messrs Buffett and Munger. Some of these are probably so deeply ingrained in me by reading them over and over, that I cannot seem to distinguish, if I had a thought prior to reading these gentlemen or if it was implanted in me post reading. So I don't make any claims on bringing original thoughts. Rather I hope I have reasonably coherently laid out the result of my synthesis of thinking about Berkshire and that this book is of use to a few.

BERKSHIRE HATHAWAY : FRAMEWORK TO CONSIDER

Berkshire Hathaway's holdings can be classified into three categories:

1. Permanent holdings
   All subsidiaries would be grouped in this classification. These subsidiaries and businesses will be continued forever unless extreme conditions cause berkshire to exit them.
2. Near Permanent holdings
   Berkshire's major stock holdings like The Coca-Cola Company, Bank of America(and possibly Wells Fargo) and Apple would be classified as near permanent holdings. It is highly likely Berkshire would continue to hold these(even possibly adding to them, if markets fluctuate to the extremes, provided there are no investment considerations, like prior approval for banking holdings increase.
3. Tradables
   Cash, All other marketable securities and bonds, treasurys and the equivalents would be classified as tradeables. Berkshire would continue to hold a considerable amount of these.

Some of the businesses are primarily based in US and few of these are international in nature.
Regardless these businesses likely will grow their footprint, in time.

In thinking about operational subsidiaries of Berkshire Hathaway, it helps to recognize that it is a conglomerate that operates across these verticals:

1. **Insurance**: P/C including Geico, BHHC, Reinsurance companies under National Indemnity group of insurance companies,
2. **Energy**: BHE, Pipelines, others
3. **Retail & Manufacturing**: FM, Borsheims, See's Candies, Diary Queen, Iscar, Mormon, others
4. **Transportation**: BNSF, Netjets, PilotJ, McLane
5. **Aerospace & Chemicals**: Precision Castparts, FlightSafety, Lubrizol, Duracell
6. **Housing**: Clayton, Berkshire Hathaway HomeServices, Roofing, Shaw Industries, Benjamin Moore
7. **Marketable Securities Permanent Holdings**:
    a. **Beverages**: The Coca-Cola Company
    b. **Banking**: BAC, WFC
    c. **Consumer electronics**: Apple
    d. **Credit card processor**: American Express
8. **Investment portfolio**: Cash, Marketable Securities and Bonds, Treasurys and the equivalents.

CONSIDERATIONS FOR INVESTING IN BERKSHIRE HATHAWAY

To consider investment value of Berkshire we have to individually consider and evaluate the business prospects across all these verticals over time. Berkshire will continue to evolve but this framework of divvying into verticals and considering prospects for each, can be extended to include any new businesses(or verticals) it enters.

Key insight into understanding the way the Berkshire Hathaway organization has been constructed is to consider the above and observe that in each of these, Berkshire is positioned to be toll collector of each of these verticals over time.

Another important observation is that in four of the above categories, Beverages, Banking, Credit card Processor and Consumer electronics, the holdings are in the form of stocks, but given their near permanent holding nature, I opt to view these are berkshire businesses, operating in those verticals, with a share of business proportional to the holding share.

Thus Berkshire acts, to serve its holder, gain percentage of earnings rights, over a cross section of good American business and which entitles its holder, berkshire shareholders, to profit from the progress of such business over time.

In analysis of each vertical I have tried to highlight remarkable characteristics of that business /vertical as a lens through which it could be understood and with which stewardship of Berkshire of that vertical's business will be illuminated.

VERTICALS ANALYSIS

Insurance

INSURANCE

Overview

Insurance operations cover multiple lines of insurance which can be broadly classified into these categories:

- Consumer vehicles(auto/motorcycles/boats)
- Reinsurance
- Workmen's compensation and others.

This group covers several insurance companies:
GEICO, Berkshire Hathaway Reinsurance Group, General Re, Berkshire Hathaway Homestate Companies, Berkshire Hathaway Specialty, Berkshire Hathaway GUARD Insurance Companies, MedPro Group Inc, National Indemnity Primary Group, United States Liability Insurance Companies, Applied Underwriters, Central States Indemnity.

Primary advantage this group of companies provide Berkshire is that they bring in Float, money that is provided by customers of insurance business at the start or ahead of their insurance coverage period, which Berkshire then invests prudently and stewards such that operating the insurance with the expected loss ratios ends up providing a profit. Float generated has grown in size over the decades and additionally it has provided Berkshire with cheap capital, and thus has provided a means for Berkshire to leverage its capital base without usual risks associated with leverage. It would be prudent to emphasis that Berkshire has been extraordinarily conservative in both operations and seeking new business and has been proven to be an excellent steward of the insurance businesses over time.

Note: Investors wishing to understand float better should read the excellent treatises Berkshire Hathaway Chairman has written in annual reports.

BEDROCK PRINCIPLE ACROSS INSURANCE PORTFOLIO

Insurance companies across the Berkshire portfolio are remarkably consistent in following one critical principle:
They do not go chasing business over profitability.
In other words every Berkshire insurance business would forego writing business if it deems the business would not be profitable. This principle alone, probably makes Berkshire's insurance vertical stand out.
This also means that Bershire's principals have chosen to weather huge fluctuations in premium volume over time in the interest of building a remarkably profitable enterprise.

ANALYSIS OF ONE COMPANY IN INSURANCE VERTICAL, GEICO

Examination of one business in this vertical, Geico shall prove to illustrate and illuminate this stewardship. Full acquisition of Geico was completed in 1996.

Geico has a virtuous business model as illustrated by the diagram below:

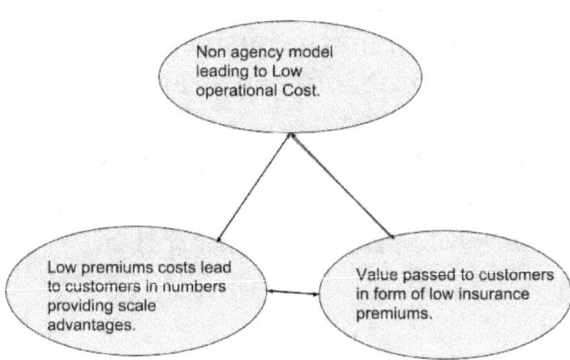

Bedrock of the business model for geico is its non-agency(i.e no intermediate commision earning agents) model allowing it to be the lowest cost operator. This enables lowest(or near lowest) costs leading to customer buy in at scale. Scale again enable further reductions of premiums over time as it allows spreading business costs over a larger customer base. Thus the virtuous business model is a self forward propelling automaton.

During the period of Berkshire's stewardship Geico has gone from strength to strength as a business as demonstrated by several dimensions of its business. First its share of customer base has steadily increased over time. Its combined ratio(includes cost of operation) has remained in range with much of the period yielding profit on float money. Geico has expanded its customer service operations, expanded territory, taken market share from competitors to move up the insurance rankings, expanded float, provided excellent service with high levels of satisfaction and expansion into adjacent lines of business coverage(bikes, rv etc). It has continued to plough in marketing dollars while its competitors have shown tendencies to curtail such spending during periods of stress.

Remarkable is also the management stability provided in the form of one steward for the business at the helm for decades(e.g. Tony Nicely) while other companies have had change of personnel. During this period there was also a remarkable investment professional(lou Simpson) who handled Geico's investments with very good results, though he has since retired.

Geico thus by any business measure has continued to imbibe strength and has shown signs of continuing to grow its already formidable business moat over time.

Potential risks for this vertical over time

- Float could reduce
- Self driving cars could lead to disruption of insurance premiums.
- Distracted driving caused by new gadgets could for ever increase accidents.
- Cost inflation

ENERGY

OVERVIEW

Energy operations cover multiple horizontals
- Utilities
- Pipelines
- NGL gatherers

The include the following companies: PacifiCorp, MidAmerican Energy, NV Energy, Northern Powergrid, Northern Natural Gas, Kern River Gas, AltaLink, BHE Renewables, BHE U.S. Transmission, CalEnergy Philippines, MidAmerican Energy Services.

Primary advantage of Berkshires energy business is twofold: First is excellence in operational excellence leading to being the lowest cost operator and long term planning with ability to commit huge sums and work with governments agencies in mutual benefiting manner with proven record over time in all regions of operations.

Analysis of one company in energy vertical, MidAmerican Energy

MIdAmerican has a diversified energy generation portfolio covering several feed types:
1. Wind,
2. Coal, Natural gas,
3. Hydro and
4. Biomass.

It is also heavily leading a push into renewables and at the same time one of the lowest cost operations among utilities resulting in providing low energy cost for middle american states.(Iowa, Illinois, South Dakota and Nebraska).

MIdAmerican has excellent safety record combined with outstanding long term record of satisfied customers and regulators across the states it has been operating in. Its website provides that as of 2017 end, it serves electricity and natural gas for 11.8

million customers across 18 states and 3 other countries(UK, Philippines and Canada).

It also has proven to be dependable capital deployer for Berkshire over time, consuming great amounts of cash for its capital projects and generating a fair return for Berkshire in turn, for its use of money.

While growing megawatts generated(owned or contracted), it has also maintained low cost operational efficiency, expanded its generational capacity to rhyme with time, with focus on renewables, expand into three countries and maintain exceptional safety at its forefront, resulting in strengthening business franchise over time.

Futhermore it has expanded into pipelines(Kern etc) and also grown mortgage brokerage services(Would not be surprised if this operation becomes the biggest brokerage service in that space, in USA, over time)

The following highlights Berkshire Hathaway Energy's moats:

Bala Thiruppanambakkam

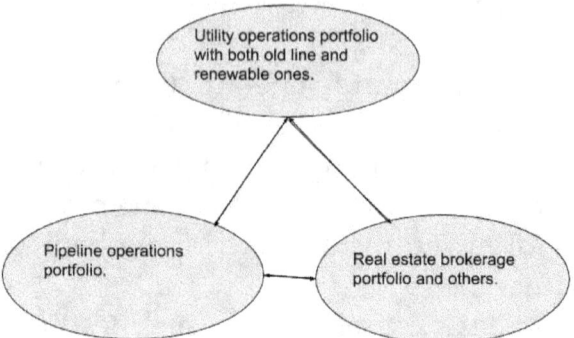

Potential risks for this vertical over time

- Hacking by foreign or home grown anarchists leading to disruption of service or more
- Potential calamities like fire triggered by utility owned facilities during disruptions caused by natural calamities(earthquake etc)
- Bursting of pipeline or gris issues leading to damage.

MANUFACTURING & RETAIL

OVERVIEW

Berkshire's operations in this space run the gamut of companies across several lines of business. Berkshires retail spans several areas: Furniture, Jewellery, Candy, Auto Dealerships, Fast Food etc. This group comprises both fully owned(and operated) as well as franchised ones.

Individual companies in the berkshire fold comprising these include:

Ben Bridge Jeweler, Berkshire Hathaway Automotive, Borsheims, Dairy Queen, Helzberg Diamonds, Jordan's Furniture, Nebraska Furniture Mart , Oriental Trading, Pampered Chef , R.C.Willey Home Furnishings, See's Candies, Star Furniture etc.

The following diagram capture Berkshires moats in manufacturing and retail.

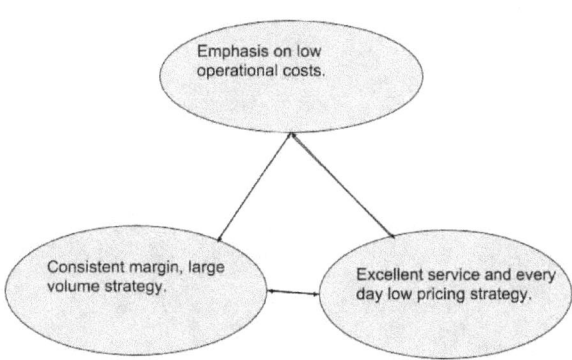

Potential risks for this vertical over time

- Cheap imports in furniture business displacing established Berkshire businesses.
- Food safety issues with those involved in making food products like, Diary Queen and See's candies

TRANSPORTATION

Overview

Berkshires operations in this vertical cover several fronts:
1. Transportation of freight/goods : BNSF
2. Transportation for high networth individuals and families(Netjets)
3. Transportation of fuel(PilotJ)
4. Transportation of retail(Mclane)

BNSF operates a sprawling network of rail across which it transport freight.

Under Berkshire umbrella, BNSF has flourished and has spent a ton of capital improving its already good rail track network and worked hard towards removing bottlenecks(especially seasonal ones). BNSF has outspent other railroads during this period of Berkshires stewardship in terms on money spent on improving its network(depreciation etc) while also achieving the remarkable record of improving its safety record.

THE FOLLOWING DIAGRAM CAPTURES SALIENT HIGHLIGHTS OF BERKSHIRES TRANSPORTATION OFFERINGS:

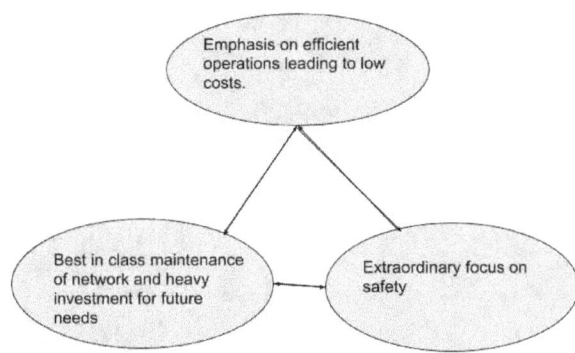

Mclane provides groceries and service supplies across vast retail footprint.

Netjets will continue to provide best in class transportation for high networth segment of population(and to businesses).

I have chosen to group PilotJ in this vertical as it is my belief that PilotJ will expand its fuel services over time to become one of the top fuel providers.

Bala Thiruppanambakkam

Potential risks for this vertical over time

Netjets might be affected if self propelled autonomous flying vehicles become ubiquitous but I do not see it happening in a short time horizon.

AEROSPACE & CHEMICALS

Overview

Berkshires footprint of companies here span from aerospace parts manufacturer to flight trainer company to chemicals manufacturers. These include

- Precision Castparts
- FlightSafety
- Lubrizol
- Duracell

Aerospace manufacturing has a huge moat in terms of entry and so does flight safety for flight training.

Lubrizol and Duracell have durable, consistent business that are decently profitable.

The following diagram highlights moats for Berkshires Aerospace companies:

Berkshire Hathaway: An Opinionated Analysis

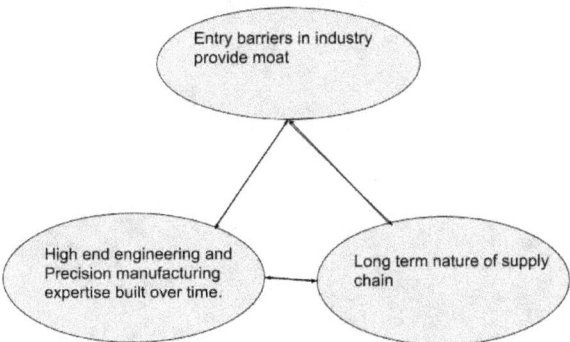

Potential risks for this vertical over time
- Drastic changes in battery technology

HOUSING

Overview

Gamut of companies under the housing vertical run across several lines:
- Clayton, builds and sells manufactured/modular/mobile homes
- Berkshire Hathaway HomeServices, provides home buying services
- Shaw Industries, manufactures carpets
- Benjamin Moore manufactures paints

There are also several other like roofing and frame manufacturers that berkshire portfolio caters to.

These non glamourous businesses have shown considerable resiliency and will ebb and flow with the housing cycle but will provide to be long live businesses that earn decently over time.

In addition in manufactured housing Berkshire provides limited financing through its subsidiaries in that space.

Berkshire Hathaway HomeServices has consistently grown under Berkshires stewardship.

My guess is that it will end up being the biggest in its space over time.

THE FOLLOWING HIGHLIGHTS BERKSHIRE'S ADVANTAGES IN THIS VERTICAL:

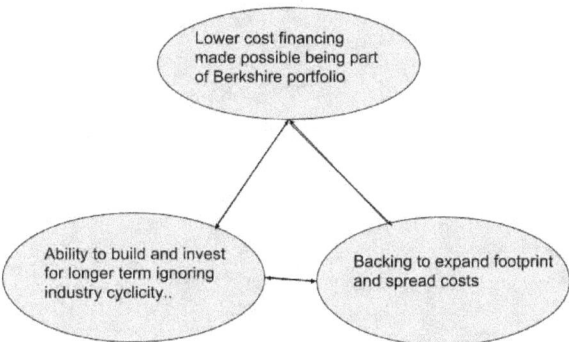

Potential risks for this vertical over time

- 3D printing taking over manufactured housing or such new technology disruption happening in a short time frame. (However if it happens at a slow pace over time, Berkshires portfolio companies can adjust and shift)

MARKETABLE SECURITIES: PERMANENT HOLDINGS

This section deals with permanent(or nar-permanent) holdings of Berkshire Hathaway held in the form of marketable securities. The main holdings here spans across the following verticals:

    a. **Beverages**: The Coca-Cola Company
    b. **Banking**: Bank of America, Wells Fargo
    c. **Consumer electronics**: Apple
    d. **Credit card processor**: American Express

Berkshire has held some of these for decades and my guess is all of the above will be continued to be held for decades hence.

One truth that is very important to observe in the above is that, over times, across all the verticals above, the investees have shown remarkable franchise and moat growth in their respectable businesses.

Berkshire's proportional share of these businesses will grow with their business growth as well as share repurchases.

Over time across banking, beverages, consumer electronics and credit card processing network verticals Berkshire will become a considerable tollkeeper by virtue of these holdings.

The following diagram captures essential features that distinguish these marketable security holdings classified as (near) permanent holdings:

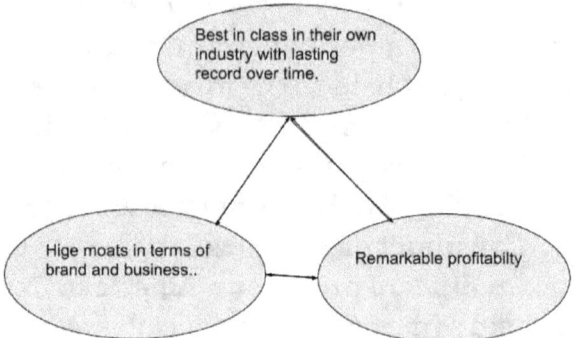

INVESTMENT PORTFOLIO

This consists of Cash, Marketable Securities and Bonds, Treasurys and the equivalents. Consider all held under this umbrella, except for 20 Billion, which is cash equivalents Berkshire has promised to hold onto to weather through extreme catastrophes. Over time this amount could increase a bit more. So evaluation should be made with that in mind.

INVESTMENT CONSIDERATIONS: EVALUATION FOR INVESTMENT UNDERTAKING

First I will lay out considerations one has to keep in mind before any investment decision.

A company, from a shareholders perspective, exists primarily to perform these functions:
1. Generate excess cash.
2. Deploy all or a portion of this cash generated with good return on capital employed.
3. Return the excess cash that cannot be deployed intelligently.
All of the above have to be evaluated over a long period of time to be reasonably certain if a company is a worthwhile economic investment for a person investing.

Generating excess cash

Economics of an underlying business dictates to a large measure, if a company can over time, generate excess cash. A great manager could definitely make a difference but the difference arises mainly by reuse of cash generated to deploy to a more advantageous business rather than drastically changing the whole economics of an industry by business model disruption.(Except for outliers).

There are three primary factors to consider with regards to the ability of a company to generate excess cash.
1. Opportunity cost
2. Return on that capital
3. Business model disruptions in industry

Opportunity cost

The only consideration(important) in business capital employment is evaluation of opportunity costs in capital deployment, with a record over time, indicating clear judgement ability, to deploy effectively.

Opportunity cost evaluates and compares merits of one investment over the other and quantifies them based on investment considerations resulting in a raked order of investment preferability.

A thorough business analysis is a prerequisite towards intelligently considering and arriving at an opportunity cost of a business

Capital

Cost of capital for a business, over time, tends to factor in the business economics. Of course regulation, taxation and such risks remain but these exist for every company in that industry and tends not to overly skew results for one particular company. The conclusion I have made based on the reasoning above is there are primarily these classifications that can be made of companies based on their cost of capital.

Negative Cost of Capital companies

These are companies that get money lent/forwarded to them in advantageous terms, provided they are prudent custodians of it, deployment of which further generates additional capital, that can be used for the company's benefit.

An example would be a service for which you pay ahead of time, insurance company, which generates float in the form of car insurance premiums paid ahead of time.

Normal cost of capital companies

All the others that don't have this advantage. The sources and sustainability of cost of capital should be **qualitatively** considered as one of the inputs for the company under consideration.

Return on capital employed

Return on that capital should be **quantitatively** considered over a reasonable period of time. These can be determined from annual financial reported numbers, after necessary adjustments or perhaps from a service like valueline.

One thing to note while evaluating return on capital is that the period chosen should be reasonably long enough and should be representative of normal business climates.i.e periods of exuberation or depression might not be representative and should probably be discounted or adjusted.

Business model disruptions in industry

A good understanding of business models for the industry in which a company operates should be considered carefully. This varies by industry and in many industries can be determined with reasonable probability. Choosing an industry where business model disruption is a low probability is prudent.

Note that all the above pertain to thoughts about evaluating a company. For you to invest in it you must consider additional factors like interest rate. A complete reading of annual letters of both Messrs Buffett and Munger would help form an understanding in this regard.

In my opinion, best way to consider evaluating Berkshire Hathaway is to treat it as a conglomerate of conglomerates.

BERKSHIRE : INVESTMENT CONSIDERATIONS ANALYSIS

Berkshire principles and model: A discussion

Berkshire Hathaway is a unique company that operates on these broad principles:
1. Centralized control of earnings and careful stewarding of its deployment in sensible extensions of owned business or careful venturing into newer business, only when a margin of safety is considerable.
2. Decentralization of business operation and execution to each business unit with full power given to the business head.
3. Conservative handling of risk avoiding leverage across entirety of its businesses and prudence to carry excess cash to tide over once in 100 year worst case scenarios.

Berkshire will continue to operate on this model.

The most important benefit of this model of extreme delegation is the decision making velocity made possible for the business, at local management level, constrained only by the business leaders responsible for operating the business.

One additional benefit is operational continuity, subject to the desire of the business leaders themselves, providing them to decide and act upon their retirement planning purely based on their ability and needs.

Sources of Capital: Analysis

Berkshire Hathaway has these primary sources of capital.

1. Float money generated by insurance companies owned.

    (Example of float: Car insurance premium which you pay to your insurer ahead of time, which is used to pay the companies expenses)

2. Cash returned
    a. by operating companies
    b. from investments(dividends paid or investments sold)

3. Debt borrowing by placing bonds(or other such instruments) in market.

Berkshire has only used debt borrowing very sparingly and is very conservatively expanded its footprint over time by using float and cash returns of operating companies(and investments).

Float

Float is a very large percentage of capital for berkshire. Since for the vast majority of capital today comes in, in this form and has had a long term record of profitable underwriting, this has proven to be a considerable and sustainable advantage for Berkshire Hathaway.

A large portion of this float(car insurance premiums) also has the advantage of being mandated by insurance law and is very likely to stay this way. Furthermore this also means a large proportion of this float comes in with reasonable certainty even during stressed economic times and thus provides an advantage over other companies in such times of economic hardships.

This float and its intelligent deployment have provided Berkshire with a huge advantage primarily due to deployment skills exhibited.

Berkshire hathaway has two kinds of float from its insurance operations.

- Float generated by Reinsurance companies
- Float generated by non-Reinsurance companies(cash generated and sent to headquarters for deployment)

Float generated by Reinsurance companies should be more stable over time and grow as it has done historically. Only adverse thing on the horizon on this front is the consolidation that seems to be underway on the lower end reinsurance companies but the effect of these should be minimal.

Innovations happening in car industry(driverless, navigation etc) will probably have an effect of float generated by non-Reinsurance companies. Effects of these innovations will be playing out over the next few years and cannot be determined reasonably at this point in time except that they will probably move the float available downward.

Cash returned

Cash returned from both operating companies and investments could be reasonably determined as Berkshire has a set of companies that will endure. Investments, since these are along conservative lines, should also do well over time. Both these should trend upward at reasonable rates of return.

Deployment of incremental capital for several Berkshire Hathaway owned subsidiaries has been encouraged and should take care of keeping the earnings stream in a healthy flow.

In addition given the quality of Berkshire Hathaway's public investments(stocks) it would be reasonable to assume the earnings from these would trend upward.

Debt borrowing

By publicly committing to hold cash in excess of needs or mandated law requirements and following them consistently over decades, Berkshire Hathaway has created an impregnable fortress impression in real world and in mindshare. This provides advantageous in rating of the company and thus provides a benefit in debt borrowing as well.

In summary, all the above point to a sustainable advantage in terms of cost of capital. This probably give Berkshire Hathaway a considerable edge for the years ahead.

Return on capital employed

Berkshire has been benefiting enormously by the capital allocation skills of Messrs Buffett and Munger and this reflects in very good rates of return on tangible capital employed in berkshire portfolio (acquisitions and investments that have been held long term). Furthermore where they had erred, the error has been promptly addressed by reallocation of capital.

Study of numbers is left to reader as each individual might have a different quantitative minimal bar that a company must clear to be considered for ownership.(My only intent in writing this is to nudge the reader towards setting such a quantitative bar)

Business model disruptions in industry

Berkshire Hathaway, being the sprawling conglomerate spanning several industries, by nature provides an inherent stability against business disruptions in a particular industry. Furthermore since capital allocation is centralized, it allows for accommodating such disruptions by prudently reallocating capital or to invest to address these disruptions.

Diversity of the holdings of Berkshire Hathaway and the inherent stable nature of the core businesses held - Insurance(Geico for e.g.), RailRoad(BNSF), Utility(Berkshire Hathaway Energy) and the reasonable certainty of having a perpetual pipeline of considerable float provide Berkshire Hathaway with considerable advantage to continue the journey of being an investment of choice for long term holders.

Managerial Tenure Continuity

Berkshire managers have no mandatory retirement and can go on as long as they choose provided their performance is good. This leng managerial tenure is a hidden strength as it provides business with managers who deal from the strength of having experienced multiple business cycle in their business/industry have have had the chance to face down several disruptions of the business model from technology or otherwise. This makes Berkshires managerial set almost unique among big corporates and is a decisive advantage.

BERKSHIRE HATHAWAY: HOW WILL IT EVOLVE OVER DECADES FROM HERE

Berkshire Hathaway's investment model has been to patiently wait and strike in opportune moments for investing and just accumulate cash during most times. This nature, if continued, as expected, by the management succeeding Messrs Buffett and Munger should mean that earnings additions will be lumpy with lots of investments in stressed economic times followed by mild to no additions in normal or optimistic economic times.

Key insight in understanding Berkshire capital allocation principle is that it has been one of thoughtful flexibility over decades, evaluating opportunity costs against the alternatives available, rather than one of optimizing efficiency. Furthermore Berkshire has the ability to deploy in an unrestricted business canvas in that it can deploy in operating companies or securities or any other investment deemed to meet its high bar for investing. Over time this will bring about expansion of footprint in verticals already served as well as bringing Berkshire to play in new verticals.

Depreciation taken for past large acquisitions will come to an end mid way through the next decade. This will automatically result in a good bit of increase of reported earnings.

Berkshire will continue to be a cash generative machine. While a large portion of such cash generated will go towards building or expanding across verticals, it is inevitable a good sized portion also will be returned to shareholders.

Berkshire in short, in my opinion, will prove to be a safe and thoughtful custodian of investments for any shareholder. It also has the potential to outperform indices and/or individual money managers, by value of its business model and capital allocation, thereby rewarding its shareholders. It also is probably a more conservative and safer investment option compared to alternatives.

I conclude this with the thought that I hope my family continues to be part of Berkshire shareholder family for decades(and possibly generations) hence.

www.ingramcontent.com/pod-product-compliance
Lightning Source LLC
Chambersburg PA
CBHW051333220526
45468CB00004B/1616